ESSENTIALS

Key concepts and skills
Citizenship and PSHE at 11–14

CITIZENSHIP SKILLS

SIMON FOSTER

Series editor: John Foster

Collins
An imprint of HarperCollins*Publishers*

CONTENTS

Page	Unit	Citizenship framework coverage	Scheme of work units
3	How to use this book		
4	Becoming an active citizen		
6	Your rights and responsibilities at school	1a, 2c, 3a	1, 14
8	School councils	1a, 1c, 2a, 3c	1, 14
10	The school and the community	1f, 2a	8, 18
12	Schools and charities	1f, 2a, 3b	1
14	What makes a good neighbour?	1g, 2a, 2b, 3a, 3b	1, 13
16	Identifying community needs	1c, 2a	2, 8
18	Campaigning and taking action	1c, 2a, 3b, 3c	2, 8, 15
20	You and your local council	1c, 2a, 3b, 3c	7
22	Living in a diverse society	1b, 2a, 3b	4
24	Rejecting racism	1a, 1b, 2a	4
26	Giving young people a voice	1a, 1d, 2a, 3c	6, 12
28	Political parties	1d, 1f, 2a, 2b, 3b	6, 12
30	Voting and elections	1d, 1e, 2a, 2b, 3b, 3c	6, 12
32	You and your MP	1c, 1d, 2a, 2b	6, 12
34	Children's rights	1a, 1f, 2a, 2b, 2c	3, 16
36	World problems	1i, 2a, 2b, 2c	10, 17
38	Becoming a global citizen	1i, 2a	10, 11, 13
40	Debating global issues	1i, 2b, 2c, 3a, 3b, 3c	10, 11, 13
42	The media – news stories	1h, 2a, 3a	9
44	The media – pictures	1h, 2a, 3a	9
46	Being a volunteer	1f, 2a, 3b, 3c	14, 19
48	Glossary		
49	Acknowledgements		

HOW TO USE THIS BOOK

This book contains information, advice and suggested activities designed to help you develop your citizenship skills. To learn more about what these skills are and why they are important, read 'Becoming an active citizen' on pages 4–5.

Features

Each self-contained unit in this book features some or all of the following:

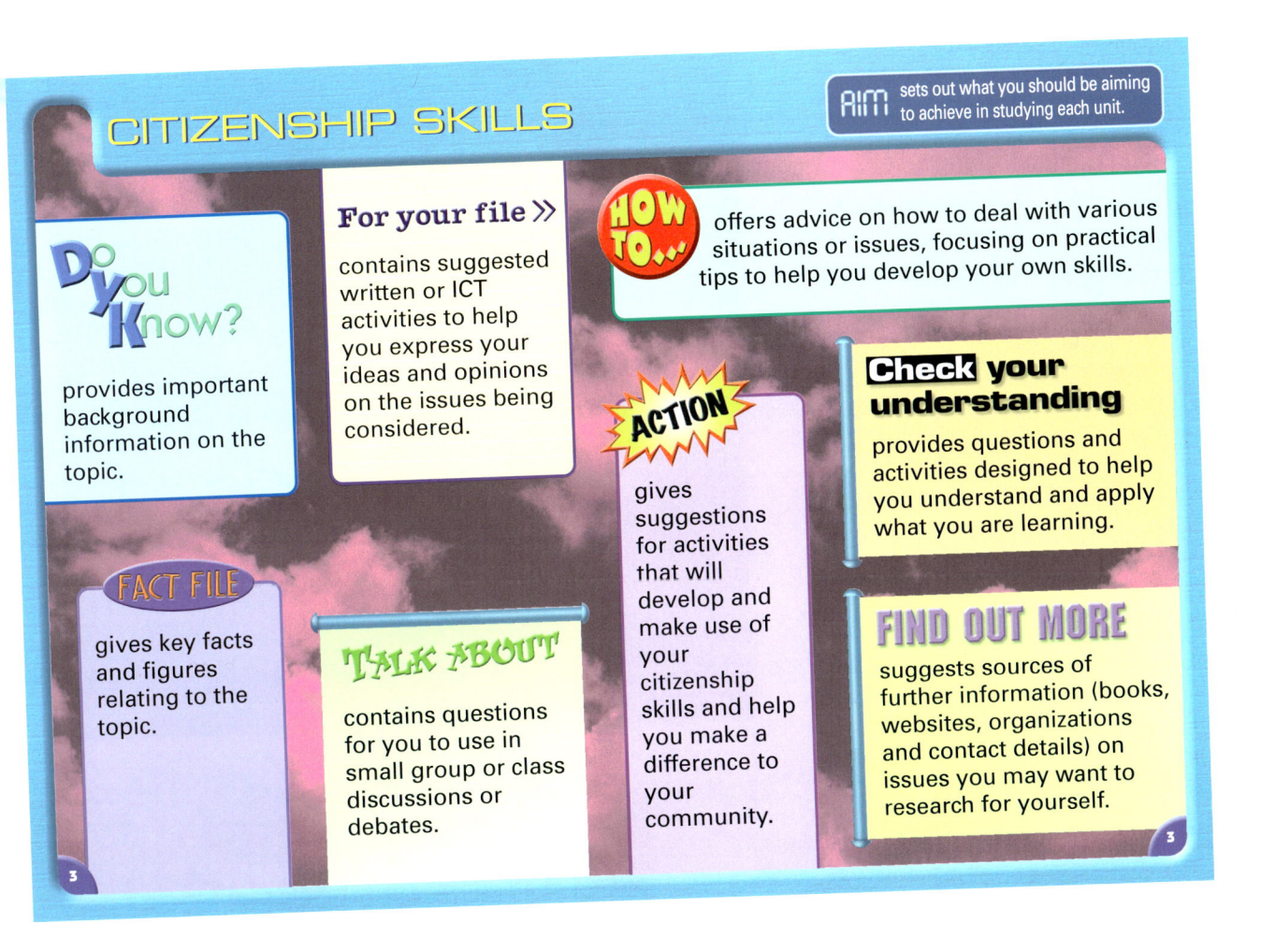

CITIZENSHIP SKILLS

Aim sets out what you should be aiming to achieve in studying each unit.

Do You Know? provides important background information on the topic.

For your file contains suggested written or ICT activities to help you express your ideas and opinions on the issues being considered.

HOW TO... offers advice on how to deal with various situations or issues, focusing on practical tips to help you develop your own skills.

Check your understanding provides questions and activities designed to help you understand and apply what you are learning.

FACT FILE gives key facts and figures relating to the topic.

TALK ABOUT contains questions for you to use in small group or class discussions or debates.

ACTION gives suggestions for activities that will develop and make use of your citizenship skills and help you make a difference to your community.

FIND OUT MORE suggests sources of further information (books, websites, organizations and contact details) on issues you may want to research for yourself.

BECOMING AN ACTIVE CITIZEN

Do You Know?

What is an active citizen?

Here are some views on what being an active citizen means.

1. Knowing your rights and being prepared to stand up for them.
2. Understanding that you have responsibilities towards other people.
3. Keeping yourself informed about what's going on in the world.
4. Getting involved in the life of the school and the local community.
5. Respecting people's differences and speaking out against racism, intolerance and injustice.
6. Working with other people to bring about changes in our society.
7. Using your vote to choose people to represent you on your local council and in Parliament.
8. Taking part in discussions and debates about important issues and expressing your views about what should be done.
9. Knowing who to contact about issues and problems and taking the initiative to contact them.
10. Understanding how news is presented on the media and how the media can be used to campaign for change.

Talk About

Study the list of statements above. What do they tell you about what people think being an active citizen involves? What do *you* think being an active citizen means?

Why citizenship skills are important

It is important to develop your citizenship skills for several reasons:

- It can give you a better understanding of the society in which we live.
- It can enable you to know how to make the world you live in a better place.
- It can broaden your experiences and help you to develop skills you'll need in your adult life.

Aim: To explore what being an active citizen means and what skills are required for active citizenship.

Developing your citizenship skills

In order for you to be able to play a full part in society the Citizenship curriculum is designed to help you learn:

- what your rights and responsibilities at school are
- how you can be involved in making decisions about school matters, and how to choose people to represent you on a school council
- how your school can help the wider community, for example by fundraising for charity
- what being a good neighbour involves
- how you can get involved in projects to improve the local area
- what your local council does and how you can raise an issue with the local council
- that we live in a diverse society in which everyone has a right to equal opportunities and that it is your duty to stand up against racism, prejudice and discrimination
- that Britain is a democracy, how everyone over 18 can share in choosing the government by voting and that young people can make their voice heard in a number of ways, including contacting their MP
- that Britain is one of the states within the world community of states, each of which has responsibilities towards each other
- that international issues are of concern to everyone and that we need to work cooperatively to try to solve the world's problems
- how to keep informed about local, national and international affairs, how news is brought to us by the media and how to detect bias in both words and pictures.

Three young people talk about what they gained from getting involved as active citizens:

I learned a lot from being on the school council. It helped me gain confidence. I got a real buzz from playing a part in getting more facilities for our Year group to use at breaktimes.

I joined the action group to campaign for a swimming pool in our town. I helped to distribute leaflets and even went to a council meeting. It was interesting to see how decisions are made.

I volunteered to help clean up a path where people had been dumping their rubbish. It was disgusting, but it's great to see people using the path again. I made some good friends.

TALK ABOUT

1. Discuss ways that you can develop your knowledge and understanding of:
   a) local affairs
   b) national affairs
   c) international affairs.
2. Talk about how often you read newspapers and watch TV news and current affairs programmes. What could be done to make news broadcasts more interesting so that young people would take more notice of them?

5

YOUR RIGHTS AND RESPONSIBILITIES AT

Do You Know?

What rights do you have at school?

As a member of your school, you have certain **rights**. Here's what some pupils said when asked to talk about their rights at school.

> We've the right to move round the school without feeling threatened or frightened.
> (Alma)

> We should be able to decide for ourselves whether or not to attend lessons.
> (Mike)

> We've the right to get on with our work without being disturbed.
> (James)

> We should have the right to choose who we sit next to and work with in class.
> (Tariq)

> We should have the right to wear whatever we like to school.
> (Simone)

ACTION

In groups, discuss what rights and responsibilities you have in lessons. Then write out a classroom code of conduct giving guidelines for responsible classroom behaviour.

What is your responsibility outside school?

I was told off in front of the whole class because a shopkeeper complained about the way I was behaving in his shop on my way home from school. The Head of Year said I was letting myself and the school down because I was in school uniform. She said it's my responsibility to behave well whenever I'm in school uniform. I don't think it's fair to be told off at school for how I behave outside school.

(Carla)

Talk About

Your rights at school. Say whether you agree or disagree with the views above on your rights at school. Draw up a list of what rights you think school pupils should have. Then compare your views in a class discussion.

Your responsibilities at school. Having rights means having responsibilities about how to behave. Draw up a list of your responsibilities at school. Then compare your lists in a class discussion.

School rules. What is the purpose of school rules? Imagine you are a committee who have been asked to draw up the rules for a new school for 11–16-year-olds. Draft your list of school rules, then compare it to your own school's rules.

Talk About

In pairs, discuss what happened to Carla. Do you think it was right for the school to tell Carla off? Would it have made a difference if Carla had been on a school trip when a similar incident occurred?

SCHOOL

AIM To explore your rights and responsibilities at school.

What is responsible behaviour?

In some situations it can be difficult to decide what is the right thing to do. One of the unwritten rules of friendship is that we should always be loyal. But what happens if you find your friend doing something wrong? Your loyalty to your friend may conflict with your **responsibilities** towards others and to the school community as a whole.

Similarly, there is an unwritten rule about telling tales. It's all very well not telling if you see something minor happening, but what happens if you see something happening which is likely to have serious consequences if it is not reported or stopped? It can be difficult to decide when to speak out, because your responsibility to tell is more important than being branded a 'sneak'.

CASE STUDY 1

Pat is in your class. You get permission to go into your classroom at break one morning to get a book you want to look at before an exam that afternoon. You find Pat standing at the teacher's desk. She's found the exam paper and is reading it. Pat says that if you tell, she'll say you were cheating too. You do the exam and Pat comes top. Should you say anything?

CASE STUDY 2

There has been some vandalism in the bike sheds. You are on your way back into school from the dentist's and you see a gang of Year 10 boys doing something to a bicycle. You know that they shouldn't be there because most of them come to school on the bus. You're frightened of them, but it's been pointed out at assembly how dangerous it can be if someone rides a damaged bicycle without realizing. What should you do?

CASE STUDY 3

You always used to have lunch with your friend Kim, but recently she's stopped coming into the canteen. You can tell something is worrying her. You ask her what's wrong and she says she'll tell you on condition that you don't tell anyone else. You find out that two Year 11 pupils are bullying her and taking her dinner money. One of the Year 11 pupils is a friend of your brother's and comes round to your house quite often. Now that you've found out what's going on, what should you do?

CASE STUDY 4

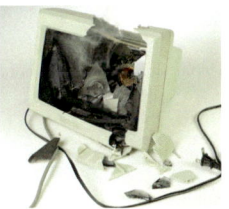

A piece of equipment has been broken in the IT room. The teacher says that unless the person owns up, the whole class will have to stay in at break. You saw it happen and know who was responsible. You're worried about being kept in because there's an important team meeting at break and your PE teacher has warned you that anyone who doesn't attend will be dropped from the team. When the bell goes, the person still hasn't owned up. What do you do?

For your file »

Write a story based on an incident at school in which a pupil is faced with a difficult choice and must decide on the most responsible way to behave. You could give your story two different endings to show the consequences of the different decisions the pupil could have made.

TALK ABOUT

In groups, discuss what you would do in each case and share your views in a class discussion.

SCHOOL COUNCILS

Do You Know?

What is the aim of a school council?

A **school council** is a committee of representatives. It meets regularly to discuss school issues, to make suggestions to improve the running of the school and to organize activities. The aim is to give everyone in the school community a say in the running of the school. So the representatives usually consist of pupils from each Year group, teachers and, sometimes, parents.

What issues should a school council help to decide?

> Obviously there are certain important matters that must be decided by the teaching staff, the governing body and the local education authority. The school council can only be involved in decision-making in certain areas.
> (Headteacher)

> It's our school. We have the right to be consulted and to help to make decisions on all matters that concern us.
> (Jez)

School council: issues for discussion

1. School discipline and the detention system
2. The school curriculum
3. School uniform
4. School twinning arrangements
5. School term dates and school holidays
6. Antibullying and equal opportunities policies
7. Fundraising activities
8. Transport to and from school
9. School outings and social events
10. Breaktime and lunchtime arrangements
11. The school environment
12. Use of the school premises by the local community
13. Extracurricular activities and clubs
14. The purchase of new books and equipment
15. Decoration of the school premises

Talk About

1. Who should have representatives on the school council? Should it be just teachers and students? Should there be parent representatives? What about other members of the school community – teaching assistants, administrative staff, caretaking staff, school governors? What about members of the local community, for example taxpayers, whose money funds the cost of education? Or local neighbours whose houses are next to the school and its grounds? Imagine you are drawing up the constitution for your school council, and decide who its members will be.

2. In groups, study the list of issues which a school council could discuss. On which issues do you think the school council should be able to:
   a) have a say?
   b) help make decisions?

Aim: To discuss what school councils do and to choose representatives for your school council.

Choosing your representatives

Hold an election to choose someone to represent your class on the school council. The following 'job description' might be useful:

School council representatives must be able to do all of the following:

- attend school council meetings, listen to others and contribute to discussion
- listen to the views of your class and share them with the school council
- take part in assemblies and class councils and tell your class what the council has discussed
- keep your form room school council noticeboard up-to-date
- act on decisions the school council make
- take part in action research
- have good punctuality and attendance
- promote good learning in the classroom.

Talk About

1 In groups, think about who would make a good school council representative, considering the list (left). Then nominate candidates for the job by filling out a nomination form. (Note: each candidate should be nominated by three people for the nomination to be valid.)

> We, the undersigned, nominate Cheryl Johnson to be our class representative on the school council for the year 2003/4.
> Signed   Josie Martin,
> Sharif Mahmood,
> Elwood Powell
>
> I agree to be nominated for the school council.
> Signed   Cheryl Johnson

Who would make a good representative?

2 Ask each of the candidates to present a speech saying why they think they should be chosen as the class representative.

After each candidate has spoken, hold 'Question time' in which other members of the class can ask them questions. Then hold an election to choose your class representative.

3 In groups, discuss the key issues of concern of your class members which you would like your representative to raise at the next school council meeting. Appoint a spokesperson to tell the rest of the class which issues your group would like raised. Agree on a class list.

Find Out More

Visit school councils' websites to find out how other school councils are organized and the things that they do.

THE SCHOOL AND THE COMMUNITY

Improving the school environment

The school environment affects everyone who works there, from the headteacher to the person who cleans your classroom. Caring for the school buildings and grounds is the responsibility of all the members of the school community.

How could your school environment be improved? Here's what the pupils in one school said when they were asked to suggest ways of improving their school environment.

- Provide everyone with lockers and coat pegs so that there aren't piles of bags and coats everywhere.
- Widen the paths between buildings so that people don't step in mud and bring dirt into the buildings.
- Paint murals on some of the walls to brighten them up.
- Plant more trees around the field to provide more shade in summer.
- Replace the fencing around the playground.

Talk About

1. Discuss what could be done to improve your school environment.
2. Imagine that a former pupil of the school, now a successful businesswoman, has given a donation of £5000 to the school to be spent on 'improving the school environment'. She wants pupils to be involved in drawing up plans on how the money should be spent. In groups, discuss how you would spend the money. Then, as a class, agree and draft a proposal of how you would spend the money.

Making the school a better place

What would make your school a better place? Here's what one group of pupils wrote when asked to list three things that would make the school a better place.

Our school would be a better place if...

- people didn't push and shove in the doorways
- there wasn't so much litter everywhere
- the lunch hours were staggered for different Year groups

Talk About

In groups, decide on three things that you think would make your school a better place. Then share your ideas in a class discussion.

AIM To consider ways of improving your school environment and developing community use of the school.

Community use of the school

The wider school community includes everyone in the local area who uses the school's facilities. Many secondary schools have facilities which are used by the local community outside school hours – in the evenings, at weekends and in the holidays. For example, community education classes are often held in school buildings, and the hall and sports centre are used after school by local clubs and societies.

In some schools, where there is space available, there is community use of the school during school hours. For example, there is a crèche or nursery for the children of staff and local people.

In other schools, which lack the space to run regular activities, community events are organized on a one-off basis. For example, groups of older people may be invited to attend the dress rehearsal of a concert or school play, free of charge.

ACTION How could your class make use of the school's facilities for the benefit of the local community? Plan and organize a one-off event for members of your local community, for example a tea dance for older people.

TALK ABOUT

1 Discuss all the different uses that the local community makes of your school premises.

2 Draw up proposals for other uses that the local community might make of your school and its facilities.

SCHOOLS AND CHARITIES

What do you think about giving money to charity?

What's the point? Charities spend too much money on administration, and not enough on the causes they're supposed to help.

I think giving money to charity is a good thing.

I hate it when I see a charity collector in the street asking me for money.

Everyone should give a little bit of money to charity regularly.

You shouldn't need to give money to charity – the Government should take care of it.

I feel guilty if I don't give money to a charity when they ask.

I'll happily give money to charity, provided I have some money to spare.

ChildLine
0800 1111
Reg'd charity no.1003758

CANCER RESEARCH UK
Registered Charity No. 1089464

TALK ABOUT

On your own, look at the statements about giving money to **charity**. Say whether you agree or disagree with each statement. Then share your views in a group discussion.

Which charity would you like to support?

Look at the following list of charities. Which do you think is the most popular? Why?

- Cancer charities
- Help the Aged
- Comic Relief
- NSPCC
- Guide Dogs for the Blind
- RSPCA.

TALK ABOUT

Talk about the different charities that people like to support and discuss which type of charity *you* would like to support.

- Would you like to support a local or a national charity?
- Do you want to support a charity which helps animals or people?
- Do you want to help people who are ill or those who have disabilities?
- Do you want to help people in Britain or those in developing countries?
- Do you want to help children or older people?

Aim: To discuss giving money to charity, to choose a charity and to organize a fundraising event.

How to... organize a charity event

Decide what sort of charity event you are going to organize. It could be one of the following:

- a non-school uniform day
- a sponsored walk, run, or silence
- an end-of-term school disco
- a fête, including a raffle
- a jumble sale, selling second-hand books, clothes and toys.

Remember the aim of your event is to raise money, and the best way to raise money is to have fun. Here's a plan that you might find useful.

1. Get a group of people together who wish to help with the charity event.
2. Make a list of all the tasks that need to be completed for the event to take place.
3. Set yourself a budget. This includes all the money you need to spend on the event, and all the money you think you might raise.
4. Choose one person who will act as your event manager – their job is to delegate tasks to everyone. They will also 'chase' everyone to make sure that their tasks are completed on time.
5. Share out the tasks equally among everyone involved. Remember, your plan should be achievable – take your time and do things properly.
6. After the event, hold a review meeting. Count how much money you raised.
7. Present your donation to your charity. This could include inviting the media, to create more publicity for your charity.

Check your understanding

1. What are the different steps that you need to take to organize a successful charity event?
2. Hold a fundraising event in your local school, either an end-of-term disco, or an event of your choice.

FIND OUT MORE

Contact The Giving Campaign, which aims to get more pupils and schools involved in charity work. The Giving Campaign can be contacted at: The Giving Campaign, 6th Floor, Haymarket House, 1A Oxendon Street, London SW1Y 4EE Tel: 020 7930 3154
Email: admin@givingcampaign.org.uk
Website: www.givingcampaign.org.uk

WHAT MAKES A GOOD NEIGHBOUR?

Do You Know?

What is antisocial behaviour?

Being a good neighbour involves thinking about how your behaviour affects other people, showing respect for them and their property and avoiding **antisocial behaviour**. Here are some case studies of young people whose behaviour caused disputes with their neighbours.

> I was rollerblading along a path through the park and this young woman with a pushchair started shouting at me and called me a dangerous hooligan. (Jed)

> I was taking my dog for a walk and it did its business on this man's lawn. He went berserk and chased me down the street. (Alana)

> My friend and I are in this band and we practise in this lock-up garage belonging to my friend's dad. The man who lives opposite complained because he works nights and the noise was keeping him awake. (Naz)

> My mates and I had some chips and a drink down by the swings. When we got up to leave this old bloke started going on at us just because we left some rubbish behind. (Ali)

> I was at the bus shelter that's covered in graffiti and I was bored so I started scratching my name on it. This woman saw me and said she'd report me. (Toni)

> We were having a laugh on the bus and the bus driver threatened to put us off because we were swearing. (Conrad)

> This woman had a real go at me because I cleared my throat and spat. What's wrong with spitting? Footballers do it all the time. (Pam)

Antisocial behaviour orders

Antisocial behaviour orders were introduced in 1999 to deal with persistent and serious antisocial behaviour. Under an antisocial behaviour order a person can be banned for two years or more from areas where they have been repeatedly causing a nuisance by their behaviour.

A 16-year-old girl has been given a five-year antisocial behaviour order, banning her from parts of Portsmouth and from threatening residents and assaulting police officers.

Imposing the order, the magistrate said he had taken into account that she had been convicted of over 100 offences involving assault, disorderly behaviour, damage to property and use of obscene language.

Chief Inspector Julie Earl said she was delighted with the order. "It will help us protect people from this individual's behaviour. It prohibits her from going to locations where she has caused so much nuisance in the past."

From *The Daily Telegraph* 16 May 2002

Talk About

Discuss these case studies. Which of them do you think are examples of antisocial behaviour? What other examples of antisocial behaviour can you think of?

For your file

1. List the different types of behaviour that you consider to be antisocial.
2. What are antisocial behaviour orders? Say whether or not you think they are a good idea.
3. Write a paragraph saying what you think makes a good neighbour.

AIM To explore what antisocial behaviour is, and what being a good neighbour involves.

Getting involved in action groups

Being a good neighbour also involves getting involved in community affairs. There are a number of ways that you as an individual can become involved in doing something to improve your neighbourhood. You could either join an action group or set one up yourselves.

On this page several young people describe why they became involved in action groups and what they did to try to improve their neighbourhood.

Tamara and Tayfon got involved in schemes developed by Youth Works, a national charitable organization.

> There wasn't much to do but hang about and get into trouble until Youth Works was launched on the estate. Since then, I have been helping to set up the Youth Works Drop-in Centre and Cyber Café.
> As well as providing something useful for other young people, there is no doubt that this will help me to get some qualifications, which will make sure I get a good job.
> (Tamara, aged 14, Bridgend, South Wales)

> The most enjoyable bit was gardening and building the new playground. We came up with ideas for improving the area and everyone worked together. Some of them didn't know each other even though they live in the same place — now people from different backgrounds know each other better.
> (Tayfon, aged 16, Hackney, London)

Georgia joined a youth action group run by the National Youth Agency to campaign for a skate/BMX park.

> I got involved in my youth action group because I felt our rights were being neglected. In our town, we've got the usual problems: nothing to do, nowhere to go. The under-16s are banned from the arcades on the seafront after 7pm, which leaves the bus shelters to hang out in. Skaters always get moved on. There are no drama, dance or music facilities. The council decided to fill in the BMX trails in a nearby wood, but didn't tell us it was for safety reasons. The lack of communication between them and us meant that we had to prove that young people genuinely want something constructive to do in their spare time.
> (Georgia, aged 16, St Anne's, Lancashire)

Talk About

Discuss why Tamara, Tayfon and Georgia got involved in action groups. What did they do and how do they say they benefited from their experiences? Talk about whether you would consider joining an action group and say why.

FIND OUT MORE

1 For advice on setting up or joining a youth action group in your area, visit the National Youth Agency website: www.nya.org.uk.

2 For information on Youth Works contact the Youth Works National Development Manager, 85–87 Cornwall Street, Birmingham B3 3B, website: www.youth-

IDENTIFYING COMMUNITY NEEDS

Do You Know?

How can you find out what your community needs?

If you want to take action to improve your neighbourhood, the first step is to find out what the community needs and to identify what could be done to meet those needs.

A good way of collecting information is to do a survey. A survey is usually carried out by designing a questionnaire, and asking a number of people to answer it.

Local crime questionnaire

Elena decided to conduct a street survey on crime in her local area. Speaking to her friends and family, she found out that people thought that crime wasn't a problem in the past. She therefore designed a survey on local crime.

Name:_____
Address:_____

1) How much crime do you think there was in our village five years ago?
   A little ☐   Some ☐   A lot ☐

2) How much crime do you think there is in our village today?
   A little ☐   Some ☐   A lot ☐

3) How much crime do you think there will be in our village in five years' time?
   A little ☐   Some ☐   A lot ☐

4) Do you think there is enough street lighting in our village?
   Yes ☐   Don't know ☐   No ☐

5) Do you think there are enough police on our streets?
   Yes ☐   Don't know ☐   No ☐

6) Have you been a victim of crime in the last year?
   Yes ☐   Can't remember ☐   No ☐

7) If yes, what sort of crime?_____
   If no, go to question 8.

8) Is there anything else you would like to add to our crime survey?

Thank you very much for your time – it is appreciated.

HOW TO... conduct a fact-finding survey

1. Decide on an issue that you want to investigate.
2. Talk to people about what they feel is important.
3. Decide what information you want to get out of your survey.
4. Draw up a list of questions and possible answers for your survey.
5. Try out your survey on several people that you know, to check that your survey works. This is known as 'piloting' your survey.
6. Redraft your survey, and make any changes you think are necessary.
7. Conduct your survey.
8. Write your results in a report.

ACTION

Conduct a survey in your local area. Either use your redrafted version of Elena's crime survey or hold a survey on an important local issue, for example, a survey on people's views about the local environment or local transport.

Talk About

1. In pairs, study Elena's survey. What do you think of her questions? Do you think she has all the questions in the right order?
2. What questions would *you* ask if you were conducting a crime survey? Redraft Elena's survey. Then compare your redrafted versions in a class discussion. Decide which of your surveys would produce the most interesting information.

AIM To investigate community needs by carrying out a survey and analyzing the results.

HOW TO... analyze your survey and write a report of your findings

1. Add up the numbers for each of the answers to your questions. You can use a computer to do this.
2. Now study the results to see what they tell you. For example, the answers to questions 1–3 told Elena that people thought crime had increased in the last five years (see the table below).
3. Consider the different ways you might present the figures in your report. Elena used a table, a line graph, a block graph and a pie chart.
4. Study the answers to any open-ended questions. Do they reinforce anything that the figures show? For example, Elena found that most people in the village felt the street lighting was inadequate and Mrs Smith wrote in answer to question 8: "I'm particularly concerned about the area round the bus shelter. It's so dark at night, without adequate street lighting. I really think something should be done."
5. Pick out two or three key comments, such as this, to include in your report.
6. Draft your report. Start with an introduction saying when and where you carried out your survey, and how many people you interviewed.
7. End your report with a paragraph giving a summary of the main conclusions drawn from the results of your survey.

Different ways of presenting information

A table can be used to present the figures that you found out for several questions. Elena used a table to present the answers to her questions 1 to 3.

		A little	Some	A lot
1)	Crime in the past	15	7	3
2)	Crime now	10	5	10
3)	Crime in the future	7	3	15

A line graph can be used to present information about questions that be can be compared to one another. Looking at the table, Elena saw that there is an increase between people who thought there was a lot of crime five years ago, now, and five years in the future. She drew a line graph to illustrate this.

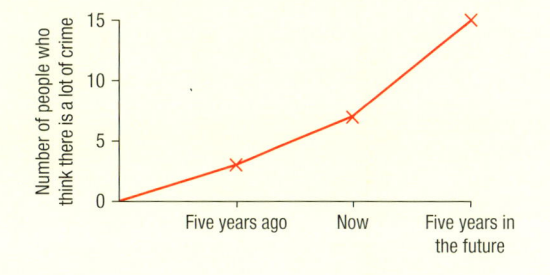

A block graph can be used to show a comparison between different answers, and even between different questions.

Elena decided to draw a block graph for questions 4 and 5, in order to show that more people were concerned about the lack of street lighting than about having more police in the village.

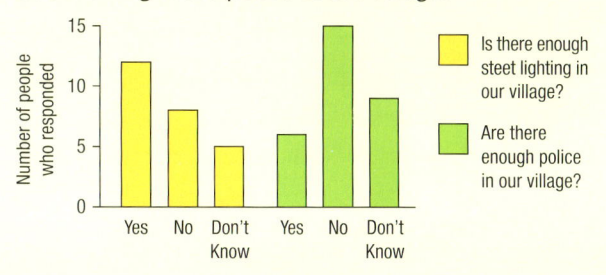

A pie chart can be used to show the different percentages in response to a question. Elena decided to use a pie chart to show the figures she obtained for question 6. Ten people said 'Yes', none said 'Can't remember' and 15 people said 'No'.

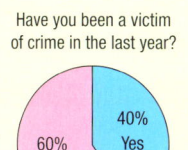

17

CAMPAIGNING AND TAKING ACTION

A campaign for better street lighting

Following her crime survey, Elena made a list of all the crime problems she would like to solve in her village. She included the lack of police, lack of street lighting, graffiti on the bus shelters, the older teenagers who hang about shouting and swearing outside the chip shop, and some vandalism to the benches in the park.

Elena then decided to prioritize her list, giving each issue a different number of points:

Lack of police	10
Lack of street lighting	8
Older teenagers who cause trouble outside the chip shop	6
Vandalism to the park benches	4
Graffiti on the bus shelter	2

Elena looked at the top three items. She knows she can write to the Government about getting more police for her village, but recognizes this is a nationwide problem. She thinks what young people need is a youth centre to keep them off the street, but doesn't think that will happen in her small village. However, she knows the local council is responsible for street lighting, so she drew up an action plan for a campaign to get the street lighting improved.

She decided she would:

1 contact the local district council and speak to local councillors about the need to improve the street lighting

2 contact the local community police officer to enlist their support for her campaign

3 write to the chair of the local parish council to ask them to raise the issue at their next meeting

4 write an article about her survey and her campaign for the parish magazine

5 send a press release about her campaign to the local radio station and the local papers

6 write a letter about her campaign to the local MP

7 draft a petition to present to the local council.

TALK ABOUT

Discuss how Elena identified her priorities and drew up her action plan. What do you think of her action plan? Suggest what else she might do.

AIM To understand how to take action to campaign for changes that will benefit your community.

HOW TO... decide on a plan of action

The list below shows a step-by-step approach to help you decide which problem to focus on and what action to take to try to get it dealt with.

Make a list of all the issues that your survey identified as problems.

- Give each item on your list points between 1 and 10 – award 1 for issues that you consider to be the least important, and 10 for the items you think are a top priority, requiring urgent action.
- Look at the top three items on your list. Pick one problem that is a priority, and that you think you could actually get something done about.
- Decide what you can do to try to get something done about the problem. For example, you could write letters, contact the local radio station, organize a petition.
- Discuss your ideas with someone else and see if they have any suggestions to add.
- Write out the list of the steps you are going to take.
- Review and update your action plan at regular intervals, for example once a fortnight, or once a month.

MAKING A VIDEO

One good way to present your views about what can be done to change and improve your neighbourhood is to make a video.

That's what the young people on the Phipps Bridge estate in Merton did. Helped by Groundwork Merton's Making Space for Youth programme, young people from the estate made a video saying what they'd like to see done to improve the area.

The video was then used to inform and influence local community groups and decision-makers. The young people went on to help with the planning, development and building of a new garden for their youth club, including a series of colourful mosaics.

ACTION

1 Draw up your own action plan. List the issues that your survey identified as ones about which people in your area are concerned. Using the 'How to decide on a plan of action' list, decide what you consider to be the most urgent problem, draw up an action plan and carry it out.

2 Plan and make a video about your neighbourhood to show the improvements you would like to see.

19

YOU AND YOUR LOCAL COUNCIL

Do You Know?

What does your local council do?

There are over 470 local councils in the United Kingdom. They have the power to make decisions on many matters which affect the local community.

- There are two systems of local government. *County councils* exist in many rural areas of England. These are responsible for education, social services, roads, the fire service and the police. Within each county council, there are a number of *district councils*. These are responsible for refuse collection, housing, local leisure facilities and local planning.

- In Scotland, Wales, Northern Ireland, London and many urban areas, there is just one council, responsible for all of the areas listed above. In some urban areas of England, such as London, these are called metropolitan councils. In other parts of the UK these are called unitary authorities.

- The head of each council is known as the mayor. This person is sometimes elected by the council. In many places now the mayor is elected by all the voters.

- Councils account for over 25 per cent of public spending in the UK.

- Local councils are funded by taxes. Almost half of their money comes from central government grants. Another 25 per cent is provided by the council tax paid by local residents and the other 25 per cent by business rates paid by local businesses.

- Councils are elected by all the local people aged 18 and over who vote – your parents and carers and all your neighbours who live in the council area. Elections for local councils occur on the first Thursday in May in the UK at least once every five years.

- Many areas also have town and parish councils. These have very limited powers, such as looking after town halls and museums.

What do councillors do?

A councillor usually represents several thousand electors. The job of a local councillor is threefold. Firstly, a councillor attends council meetings, where important decisions are voted on. They also sit on a number of committees, for example the education committee or transport committee, where detailed proposals are discussed.

Firstly, a councillor will also meet with many other people to discuss local issues in their area. These people can include council house tenants, teachers, fire officers and refuse collectors who work for the council.

Finally, a councillor also deals with the problems of electors in their area that are the responsibility of the council. For example, there may be a problem with rubbish collection, or a new pedestrian crossing may be required near a local school. If you are concerned about an issue you can take it up with your local councillor.

Check your understanding

In groups, discuss what you learn about local councils from this page. Produce a 'Test yourself' quiz, consisting of some statements about local councils which are true and some which are false, for example 'All local councils are headed by a mayor who is elected by all the local citizens' is a false statement. Swap your quiz with another group and test each other.

FIND OUT MORE

Investigate the system of local government in the UK by contacting the Local Government Association at www.lga.gov.uk.

AIM: To understand what your local council does, and how to contact your local councillor.

How to... contact your local councillor

If you want to raise an issue with your local councillor, the best way to contact them is to write to them. The address of your local council can be found either in the front of your phone book, or on the internet.

When writing to a local councillor, make sure you include the following points:

- the name and address of the councillor
- your name, address, telephone number and email address so the councillor can contact you
- a subject title for your letter
- a brief summary of why you are writing
- what you would like the local councillor to do
- why you think the local council should take this action.

Graham and Alex Baker
6 The Reeds
Newborough
NB89 9TT
Tel: 01200 987654
Email: baker@spotmail.com

Councillor A. Smith
Newborough Council
Yew Street
Newborough
NB76 0TT

7 January 2003

Dear Councillor Smith,

Re: Closure of the swimming pool in north Newborough

Following reports in the Newborough Echo, we are writing to oppose the closure of the swimming pool park in north Newborough.

Currently, there is a lack of facilities for young people in the north of Newborough. The swimming pool was well used until it was vandalized. The closure means that the nearest swimming pool is now in Oldbury, which is eight miles away. It would be impossible for most people in north Newborough to use the pool as there is only an infrequent bus service between north Newborough and Oldbury.

We would be grateful if you could pass our letter on to the next meeting of the planning committee. We would also like to invite you to our school to discuss the issue further.

We look forward to hearing from you in the near future.

Yours sincerely,

Graham Baker   *Alex Baker*

Graham Baker
Alex Baker

Youth councils

Some local councils have set up youth councils in order to involve young people more in community affairs.

> The purpose of our youth forum is to give young people a say in matters that affect them.
>
> Local councillor

Talk about

1. Does your local council have a youth council? What are the advantages of having a youth council? How should representatives to a youth council be elected? What matters should youth councils discuss at their meetings?
2. Imagine you live in an area where there is no youth council. Draft a proposal to send to the local council, explaining why you think it should set one up and how you think it should be organized.

Action

1. Look at your local newspaper. Find out what issues your local council has been dealing with recently. Are there any other issues that you would like to raise with your local councillor? Write a letter to a local councillor about an issue which concerns you.
2. Many people do not know who their local councillor is, or what they do. How do you think your local council could inform young people about what they are doing? Find out about the work of your local council and design a leaflet for young people explaining what the local council does.

LIVING IN A DIVERSE SOCIETY

How do you see yourself

Look at the following statements. How would you describe yourself? Why?

I'm Afro-Caribbean. My grandparents came from Jamaica, but I think of myself as a Londoner.
(Curtis, London)

My parents moved from Pakistan when I was young. I grew up here, so I think of myself as English.
(Fatima, Birmingham)

I was born here, and I think of myself as Irish.
(Seamus, Belfast)

We live in Northern Ireland, and all my family think of themselves as British.
(Sonia, Londonderry)

My mum's Welsh and my dad's originally from Italy, but I think of myself as British.
(Carla,

I always call myself Scottish.
(Angus, Edinburgh)

What are the benefits of living in a multicultural society?

I love eating out in London. There's so much to choose from.
(Jan Chong, Camden)

Rap man. I canna live without ma rap.
(Jacob, Leicester)

Festivals. I'm not Hindu, but it was great when the Hindus visited our school, and explained to us about Diwali – the festival of light.
(Sally, Southampton)

It would be boring if all the world was the same.
(Rose, Stirling)

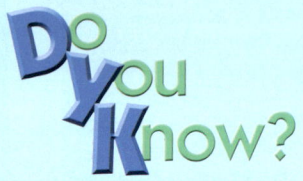

Do You Know?

How diverse is society in the UK?

The United Kingdom is a diverse society. This means that it contains many different people, from different ethnic backgrounds, who believe in different religions, and have a wide range of customs and traditions.

Because the UK is a set of islands, many groups of people from abroad have settled here over the centuries. Historians think that the earliest settlers, the Beaker People, may have come here over 4000 years ago. It is impossible for us to say who first came to the UK. Our ancestors are a mixture of people from all over Europe – Celts, Angles, Saxons, Jutes, Vikings, Normans – all of whom came here several centuries ago. They came from Africa as early as Tudor times, from Asia over hundreds of years, and even from America and the Caribbean. More recently, people escaping wars and disasters in places such as Uganda, Kosovo, Albania and Zimbabwe have come to the UK.

We use the word 'ethnic' to refer to people's languages, culture and traditions. People whose cultures are mainly found outside of the UK are called 'ethnic minorities'. However, it is important to remember that in global terms Africans and Asians are actually majority ethnic groups.

ACTION

There are many famous people from an ethnic minority background. Examples include the athlete, Denise Lewis, the broadcaster, Trevor MacDonald, and the actor Meera Syal, who stars in the television series *The Kumars at No. 42*.

Choose a person from an ethnic minority background who has made a significant contribution to society. Write about what they have achieved and say why you admire them.

Check your understanding

Describe how the UK became such a diverse society. Why have people come to the UK recently? Where have they come from? Who are the majority ethnic groups in the

TALK ABOUT

In groups, talk about the benefits of a diverse society. Think about food, music, culture, sport, travel and people. What do you like best about living in a diverse society?

Aim To understand that the United Kingdom is a diverse society, what stereotyping is and how to avoid stereotyping.

What is stereotyping?

Stereotyping is when we create an image of a group of people behaving in the same way, simply because of who they are. For example, we could say, "All asylum seekers come here for better jobs." This is clearly not true – the vast majority of asylum seekers flee their countries because of persecution, torture and murder.

Stereotyping is something we encounter every day of our lives. People often say men make better drivers, and women make better nurses. However, these broad generalizations are simply not true.

Because stereotyping involves making false assumptions, they can be dangerous. Often, we can end up treating people inappropriately, or offending someone unintentionally. The best way to avoid stereotyping is to keep an open mind.

Being stereotyped

Neelam is 13. Her family came from Bangladesh, but they now run a shop in Scotland.

"I've been called names a few times. I get the feeling people look down on me sometimes. It's like because I've got brown skin, I'm not as good as them. It's ridiculous. Customers come in the shop and talk to you like you're their slave.

"Sometimes I think people are funny towards Asians because they don't understand them. My family is Muslim. We don't make fun of Christian people or think they're weird for going to church, yet we get stared at sometimes on our way to the mosque. A few months back, the outside wall was vandalized with racist graffiti. There's no need for that. The country is big enough for everyone – why can't we all just get along?

"I'm not a criminal or a troublemaker. That's why I deserve to be treated the same as everyone else. I might have a foreign-sounding name and a different colour of skin, but underneath, I'm just the same as you."

From *Shout* Issue 134

How to... avoid stereotyping

There are several ways to avoid stereotyping. Most of them involve thinking things through carefully.

1 Don't make assumptions. Just because you have met one person who acts a particular way, it doesn't mean that everyone like them will behave in the same way. We live in a society made up of unique individuals, all of whom are different.

2 Check the facts. What somebody tells you about a group of people may simply not be true. Find out for yourself, rather than relying on others.

3 Think before you speak. Ask yourself: "Is what I'm about to say stereotyping? Is it fair?" Make sure you think things through.

4 Think about how *you* would feel. Ask yourself how you would feel if someone said: "All kids are too young to take any responsibility. You aren't old enough to do anything yourself." Stereotyping can make people feel bad about themselves and destroy their self-esteem.

Check your understanding

1 What is stereotyping? Study Neelam's story and discuss what it feels like to be stereotyped.
2 What are the best ways to avoid stereotyping?

For your file »

1 Choose a culture, investigate it and organize a week of activities to celebrate that culture, for example a Chinese week, an Arab week or an Afro-Caribbean week.

2 Find out all you can about the way of life of people from that culture – their religions, festivals and traditions, homes, family customs, clothes, food, music and sports.

3 As part of your week, you could:
   - invite people from that culture to come into school to give talks and demonstrations about their culture and lifestyle
   - put up a classroom display of posters, wall charts and artwork
   - arrange for a display of artwork and artefacts in the school entrance hall
   - arrange an evening's entertainment at which you read poems and tell stories, enact scenes, play music and perform dances from that culture
   - put on an assembly to inform the rest of the school about that culture.

REJECTING RACISM

Do You Know?

What is racism?

Racism is when you discriminate against whole groups and don't allow them their rights. This often grows out of stereotyping people according to their ethnic origin. In practice, this means treating people differently, simply because of the colour of their skin.

Many people say racism occurs when people who have power are prejudiced. Today it is generally agreed that racism is something that offends someone because of his or her ethnic identity – even if the offence is unintentional.

Look at the following case studies. Which do you think is racist? Why?

> Two school pupils discuss what a friend's parents do for a living. They discover her parents run a corner shop. Their reaction: "TP – Typical Paki."

> A young Rastafarian is not allowed to wear a hat in class, although the teacher allows a young Sikh to wear a turban.

> A group of schoolchildren are telling jokes. They decide to tell the one about the Yorkshiremen, because they all speak differently in that part of the UK.

> A young woman is refused a job in a local nightstore. The manager refuses her the job because she is white, and most people who use the store are Asian.

Now look at the checklist for racism (right). Are you surprised by anything that you read? Why?

Checklist for racism

Here are some typical racist attitudes – all of which need to be challenged.

Racism means...

- believing people from one group share characteristics, for example, 'All Chinese people gamble,' or 'All West Indians like Reggae'
- hating people from ethnic minorities and trying to force them out of the country
- expecting ethnic minorities to fit into 'the British way of life'
- white people using their power to exclude black or Asian people from opportunities for good healthcare, education and employment
- doing nothing when white people call black or Asian people abusive names
- supporting fascist organizations like the British National Party (BNP)
- blaming ethnic minorities for poor housing conditions or rising crime
- believing black or Asian people are inferior to white people – less intelligent, lazy, not capable of doing the same job
- believing that people from ethnic minorities with disabilities do not need services because 'their own people will look after them'
- black or Asian people hating white people or each other
- using words which specifically refer to people's ethnic identify in a disrespectful way, for example 'Coolie', 'Paki'
- making fun of the way people with different accents speak English.

Adapted from *What's at Issue? Prejudice and Difference* by Paul Wignall

FACT FILE

In 1976 Parliament passed the Race Relations Act to fight racial discrimination.

- This makes racial discrimination against the law, for example, in areas such as employment education, and housing.
- For housing, it is against the law for a property owner to refuse to sell or rent a house to someone on the grounds of their race or ethnic background.
- In schools, it is against the law to refuse a child a place in a school because of their race or ethnic background. Schools also have a duty to educate pupils in what it means to live in a multicultural society.
- Schools should also not discriminate against a person's language or dress. For example, Sikh boys are allowed to wear turbans, as this is part of their religion, and Muslims are allowed breaks to pray.
- At work, employers must make sure that they treat everyone fairly, whatever their race or ethnic background.

AIM To understand what racism is and the importance of taking a stand against it.

How to... stand up against racism

Speak out if it is safe for you to do so. Some racial discrimination can include offensive jokes or remarks. If it is safe for you to do so, challenge these and make it clear they are unacceptable.

Report racial discrimination. In the school, this should be to a teacher. At the workplace, this might be a manager. If the problem is serious and involves violent behaviour, the police should be contacted to investigate.

Find out what your school's equal opportunities policy is. Do you think it provides enough safeguards against discrimination? If not, suggest what might be added to it in order to make it more effective.

Conduct a survey. Often, a lot of racist behaviour goes unreported. However, by asking people if they have been the victim of discrimination, a clearer picture emerges and more incidents get reported.

Educate yourself and each other. Find out about different communities and different lifestyles. If there is a large ethnic minority population in your area, organize a talk from their community leader so you can learn more about your neighbours, and help prevent stereotyping and racism.

Challenge racism in the media

- If you think a television or radio programme is racially offensive, or if a comedian makes a racist joke or a commentator makes a racist comment, phone the company to complain. Then, make a written complaint. Send copies of your letter to the Broadcasting Standards Commission and/or the Independent Television Commission.

- If you read a racist comment in a newspaper or magazine, write to the editor. Photocopy the report or article and send them, together with a copy of your letter, to the Press Complaints Commission, the National Union of Journalists and the Commission for Racial Equality.

- Contact your local Racial Equality Council and get actively involved in their work to combat racial discrimination and make equal opportunity a reality.

FIND OUT MORE

Investigate racism and racial discrimination by contacting the Commission for Racial Equality, Elliott House, 10–12 Allington Street, London SW1E 5EH, website www.cre.gov.uk.

The Commission for Racial Equality (CRE)

The CRE was set up in 1976. It has three duties:
- to fight against racial discrimination
- to make people understand the importance of giving everyone an equal chance, whatever their race, colour, ethnic origin or nationality
- to keep a check on how the law is working, and tell the government how it could be improved.

The CRE works closely with Racial Equality Councils all over Britain and helps to fund them.

TALK ABOUT

1. What do *you* think is racist behaviour?
2. 'The media exaggerate racial problems by reporting isolated incidents of racist behaviour which suggests that racism is more widespread than it really is.' Discuss this view. How serious a problem do you think racism is?
3. Discuss the different ways of standing up against racism. Rank them in order of importance, starting with the most important, practical and effective method of combating racism. Then compare your views in a class discussion.

GIVING YOUNG PEOPLE A VOICE

The United Kingdom Youth Parliament

Everyone has the right to a say in what goes on in their Government. For people over 18 this means the right to vote, so that they can choose their government representatives, at a local, regional, national and European level.

However, people under 18 are not represented, which means that they have no real say. In order to combat this, the United Kingdom Youth Parliament (UKYP) was set up in 1999.

- There are 180 to 240 Youth Members of Parliament, or **YMPs**. Each YMP represents a **constituency** that contains a large number of schools.
- Part of the job of a YMP is to identify issues of concern for young people. For example, if there are not enough leisure centres in a constituency, the YMP then tells the people about this – local councils, political parties, and the government – to try to get something done.
- YMPs also work closely with youth groups and youth forums, to help young people gain more control over their own lives.

Voting at 16

Young people express their views on whether the voting age should be changed.

> I think 18 is the right age to start voting. You should have finished your education, before you start making decisions to run the country.

Prime Minister Tony Blair meets members of the Youth Parliament.

> You should be able to vote at 16. You can get a job and pay tax, so why shouldn't you be able to vote?

> You should be able to vote at 16, but it doesn't matter, because we've got the UK Youth Parliament, which is much better, as it concentrates on young people.

Talk About

In groups, discuss the views above. What do you think the voting age should be?

For your file »

Write about the UK Youth Parliament. Explain what it does, and say whether or not you think it is a good idea. Give reasons for your views.

Aim: To understand what the UK Youth Parliament is, and how it gives young people a voice in national affairs.

Who would make a good YMP?

Anyone aged 15–18 can become a YMP. Representatives from the schools in an area attend a training day. At the end of the day everyone votes for the person they think would best represent them in the UK Youth Parliament.

Six young people give their views about the skills they think a person needs to make a good representative as a YMP.

- They need to be good at debating and arguing a point of view.
- A good representative should be able to deal with lots of different people and respect different cultures and viewpoints.
- They need to be good at negotiating.
- Someone who has a good knowledge of current affairs, both locally and nationally.
- Someone who is persistent and doesn't give up easily.
- A person who is prepared to find things out and research what could be done about a problem.

Talk About

1. In groups, discuss the views above. Make a list of the skills and qualities you think a good representative should have. Then, compare your views in a class discussion.

2. What are the key issues which you want YMPs to raise on your behalf? What are you most concerned about: Getting the vote at 16? Changing the laws restricting the hours young people can work? Making the streets safer for young cyclists and pedestrians? Making sure young people are consulted about educational issues? Some other key issues?

   In groups, make a list of the most important issues that you would like YMPs to raise on your behalf.

Action

1. Contact the United Kingdom Youth Parliament, to find out if there is a YMP in your area. If there is, invite them to come to speak at your school, so you can learn more about their work. If there isn't, organize with the UKYP a training day for your local area, so you can elect a UKYP to represent your area.

2. Find out from your local council, teachers, or MP if there is a Youth Forum for your local area, and how you can get involved. If one does not exist, discuss setting up a Youth Forum, to represent young people in your area.

Find Out More

For further information on the United Kingdom Youth Parliament, contact www.ukyp.org.uk. For further information on the Scottish Youth Parliament, contact www.scottishyouthparliament.org.uk. For further information about changing the voting age,

POLITICAL PARTIES

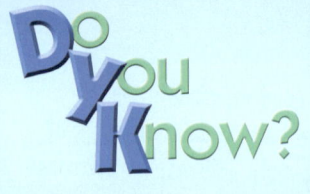

Do You Know?

What is a political party?
A **political party** is a group of people who share similar ideas about how the country should be governed. Because the United Kingdom is a democracy, we have many different political parties. We elect our Government from these political parties at elections once every five years. The party which gets the most MPs forms the Government.

At a general election each political party will produce a **manifesto**. This is what the party would do if it was in government. These are known as policies.

Form your own political party

If you were forming a political party, what policies would it have? In groups, look at the options below, and either pick one for your political party or create your own policy on that issue.

Education
Provide more money for schools by:
a) allowing private companies to take over schools and run them as businesses
b) raising taxes so that everyone pays for better schools
c) allowing parents and pupils to pay for school improvements.

Health
Provide more money for the health service by:
a) encouraging more people to have private health insurance
b) making people who smoke and/or drink alcohol pay for treatment when this makes them ill
c) raising the price of prescriptions to £10 per prescription.

Democracy
Encourage democracy by:
a) allowing everyone to vote at age 16
b) allowing everyone to vote at age 11
c) making voting compulsory for everyone aged 18 or over.

Youth crime
Reduce youth crime by:
a) spending more on youth centres, so young people have more to do at the weekend
b) allowing anyone breaking the law aged 14 or over to be dealt with in an adult court, and sent to prison if necessary
c) raise taxes so that we can have more police on our streets.

Party funding
Fund your political party by:
a) taking donations from big businesses
b) being sponsored by trade unions
c) collecting membership fees from individual party members.

Now think of at least one other policy you could have for your political party.

Choose a name for your political party. Examples from mock elections have included the 'My School Party', the 'Who Cares? Party' and the 'Vote For Me! Party'.

You could also design a logo for your political party.

Iain Duncan Smith, leader of the Conservative Party

For your file »

1. Write a leaflet publicizing your political party and summarizing its policies. You may wish to use this leaflet in a mock election campaign (see pages 30–31).

2. Contact one of the three main political parties. Find out what their main policies are and write a statement saying whether you agree or disagree with their policies. Their websites are:

The Labour Party www.labour.org.uk

Conservative Party
www.conservatives.com

Liberal Democrats
www.libdems.org.uk

AIM: To understand what political parties are and how their policies differ.

- There are three main political parties in the UK – the Labour Party, the Conservative Party and the Liberal Democrats.
- In 2003 the Labour Party had over half of the MPs in the House of Commons. This is known as a majority.
- As the largest party in the House of Commons, the Labour Party forms the Government. The head of the largest party, in this case, Tony Blair, becomes Prime Minister.
- There are also a number of other political parties. These parties tend to concentrate on one or a few different political issues. Examples include the Green Party, which campaigns on behalf of the environment, and the United Kingdom Independence Party, which campaigns for the UK to leave the European Union.
- There are also nationalist parties, which campaign for different parts of the UK to become independent. These include the Scottish Nationalist Party and Plaid Cymru, the Welsh party.
- At elections, some candidates stand as independents, which mean they are not members of a political party. However, the vast majority of MPs, councillors and elected representatives are members of a political party.

Tony Blair, leader of the Labour Party

Charles Kennedy, leader of the Liberal Democrats

Check your understanding

1. What is a political party?
2. What different political parties are there in the UK?
3. Which political party forms the Government at the moment?
4. What do you think are the advantages and disadvantages of having political parties?

HOW TO... choose which political party you support

1. Make a list of the political issues that are important to you.
2. Now put these political issues in order of priority. Start with the most important and finish with the least important.
3. Write down everything you know about the political parties you are most interested in. Check your ideas with other members of your group.
4. Compare your two lists, and see if there is one political party which you prefer.
5. You may decide you want further information before you make a decision. If so, make a list of what information you need. Then contact the political parties, either by writing to them, or by using the internet.

TALK ABOUT

1. What do you already know about each political party? In groups, compare your ideas. Does everyone have the same ideas about each political party?
2. Which political party appeals to you most? Would you ever join a political party? Why? Give reasons for your views.
3. Do you think we need new political parties to stand up for things the other parties have missed? Would they encourage more people to vote?

VOTING AND ELECTIONS

Every five years, there must be a General Election in the UK. Here, everyone over 18 elects their member of Parliament. However, at the 2001 general election, fewer than two in three people voted. In order to encourage more people to vote in the future, and to learn more about elections, schools have been holding mock elections.

HOW TO... organize a mock parlimentary election

1. Ask your teacher to act as the **returning officer**. This is the official responsible for organizing your mock election.
2. Decide when your election is going to take place.
3. Decide who are going to be the candidates in your election. Each candidate must hand in a declaration of their intention to stand to the returning officer, signed by two supporters.
4. Each candidate and their supporters should choose a political party. This can be a real party, for example the Conservatives, or you could create your own party (see pages 28–29).
5. Having chosen a party, each candidate and their supporters should discuss what their policies are and draft a manifesto saying what the candidate would do if they are elected. This should be typed on a computer and should fit onto one A4 page.
6. Candidates should also consider with their supporters how else they will try to encourage people to vote for them. This could include putting up posters, and talking to people. Interviewing people to find out how they will vote is called **canvassing**.
7. Print out and distribute copies of your manifestoes, so that everyone can read it.
8. Organize a meeting so that everyone voting can ask the candidates questions. This is known as a **hustings**. One trick at the hustings is to get your supporters to ask your opponents difficult questions.
9. Before polling day (the day of the vote) ask the returning officer to appoint people to be responsible for designing and printing the ballot papers and to provide a ballot box.
10. Also appoint two election officials who will help the returning officer oversee the voting, checking off names on the **electoral register** and ensuring that the voting is conducted fairly and in private. After voting closes, the election officials should help the returning officer count the votes.
11. The returning officer then declares the result of the election.

TALK ABOUT

Discuss what you learned about elections from holding your mock election. How did you decide who to vote for? What influenced you in the campaign? What did you think the best parts of the campaign were? Why?

FIND OUT MORE

The Hansard Society produce a mock election pack for schools. In the 2001 General Election, they helped schools run thousands of mock elections around the country. Find out more at
www.hansardsociety.org.uk/citizeneduc.htm.

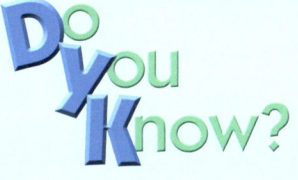

AIM To understand how we vote, and how to organize a mock election.

Do You Know?

What is an election?

In 2002, there were 659 MPs in the UK. Each MP represents an area called a **constituency** with a population of between 60–70 000 people. In order to choose an MP, you must vote. Everyone over 18 can vote in the UK.

The process of voting for MPs is called a general election. There must be a general election at least every five years. The last general election was in 2001. The next general election is expected to be in 2005 or 2006.

A person who stands for election to Parliament is known as a candidate. During an election campaign, candidates explain to people what their party will do if it is elected by distributing leaflets, holding public meetings and giving interviews on television and in the newspapers.

How do people vote?

In order to vote in a general election, your name must be on the electoral register. This is a list of people over 18 who can vote for an MP.

Voting is by secret ballot and is usually done at a polling station. Here, an official will check that you are on the electoral register. They then give you a ballot paper. This contains a list of the candidates who want to be an MP, and which political party, if any, they belong to.

You are then allowed to vote for one candidate. You do this by marking a cross in the box next to their name. The winner when the votes are counted is the candidate with the most votes.

People who can't get to the polling station are allowed to vote by post. This may include people who are working or on holiday on election day, or disabled people who can't get to the polling station. These people are also allowed to get somebody to vote on their behalf (called proxy voting). Soon voters will be able to vote using the internet.

Martin, James	Conservative	
Chowdhury, Robin	Labour	
Leigh, Amanda	Liberal Democrat	
Ashanti, Joseph	Green Party	

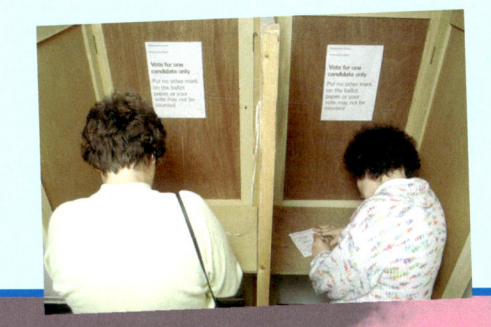

Talk About

1. Fewer than six out of every ten people voted in the 2001 General Election. This was the lowest turnout for 80 years.

   Why do you think people don't vote? What can be done to encourage more people to vote?

   Would you vote if you could? Why?

2. Say why you agree or disagree with these statements:

   Voting is pointless. The politicians don't listen to anyone, anyway. So what's the point?

   Everyone should vote. Without a vote, you don't have a voice.

   If I'm old enough to work at 16, I should be allowed to vote as well.

Check your understanding

On your own, make up a 'Test yourself' quiz about general elections and voting, for example: 'You vote by a) placing numbers by your favourite candidates; b) placing a cross by one candidate's name.' Then give your quiz to a partner to do.

ACTION

Design a poster encouraging people to vote in elections.

YOU AND YOUR MP

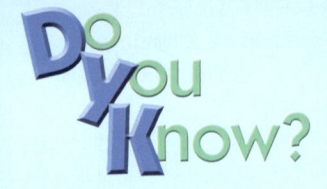

Do You Know?

What does an MP do?

Depending on which party wins the general election, an MP will be either a member of the Government or of one of the Opposition parties. If an MP belongs to the governing party, they may be given responsibility for running a Government department.

The most important MPs are the Prime Minister and the senior ministers who are members of the cabinet. These include the Chancellor of the Exchequer, who is responsible for running the country's finances, the Home Secretary, who is responsible for law and order, and the Foreign Secretary, who is responsible for foreign policy.

The main work of Parliament is to draft new laws called Acts of Parliament. As well as taking part in debates on proposals for new laws, MPs from both the Government and Opposition parties sit on committees which examine the proposed laws, known as bills, in detail.

When they are not working in the House of Commons, MPs spend time in their constituencies. All MPs have a member of staff to help people in their constituencies who have problems. These staff members are called caseworkers.

Whilst in their local area, an MP might:

- hold a surgery, like a doctors' surgery, where the MP sees people individually to discuss their problems
- attend public meetings to hear what local people have to say
- hold a question time session, where local people can ask their MP what she or he has been doing
- visit schools, hospitals, local businesses and other organizations to learn more about what is going on locally
- open a new public building, such as a school, bypass, or day centre.

Iain Duncan Smith holds a surgery.

FACT FILE

- The Hansard Society runs a campaign to help young people communicate with MPs called the 'MPs in Schools' campaign. This involves students in finding out about their MP's work in Parliament and in the constituency, deciding on a format for the MP's visit such as a question time session, a role-play or a debate, and organizing the actual visit.

- Following the success of the MPs in Schools campaign, Hansard have also set up the 'MEP in Schools' campaign. This encourages Members of the European Parliament to visit local schools to communicate with young people.

- Schools can register for these campaigns by contacting the Hansard Society at **www.hansardsociety.org.uk.**

ACTION

1. Find out who your MP is, which party they belong to, and how long they have been an MP. Find out if there are any local issues they have helped sort out in the last year. Keep a diary of your local MP's activities, and how they help people.

2. Find a local issue that you want to raise with your local MP. Contact them and arrange a meeting to express your views. Alternatively, you could invite your MP to your school to discuss a wide range of issues with your class.

Check your understanding

1. What does an MP do in Parliament?
2. What does an MP do when they are in their constituency?
3. What is the 'MP's in Schools' campaign?

Aim: To understand what an MP does, and to know how to take up an issue with your local MP.

Putting it to your MP

How to raise an issue with your MP
Barbara has learned that the Government plans to build a bypass round her town. Three different routes are proposed. Route one is through some woods where there are some badgers living, Route two is close to houses and Route three is over a bridge. Barbara decides to contact her MP to try persuade him to support Route three.

Find out the facts
She contacts the local council and discovers that the woods are classified as a 'special site of scientific interest'. This means the government thinks they are important to the environment.

She then goes to the library to read about the proposals in back copies of the local newspaper. She finds out that a pressure group of local residents has been formed to campaign to stop the bypass from being built through Route two, which they think is too close to the houses where they live.

Contact people who might help
Barbara speaks to the pressure group, who agree to campaign against Routes one and two. Route three, however, is over a river, and a bridge will cost more money.

Barbara then contacts the MP's secretary. The secretary confirms that the MP is the right person to contact. She also adds that a lot of people have written to the MP about the bypass.

Work out what you want to say
Barbara works out what she is going to say – that she wants the bypass built along Route three, not Routes one or two. She will then explain how the local woods are used by her school and other groups. Finally, she will take along the petition she, her friends and several pupils, teachers and parents have signed to present to the MP.

Practice
Barbara then practises what she is going to say, firstly alone, and then with a friend, who gives her some advice.

Visit the MP
Barbara makes an appointment to visit the MP at one of his Saturday surgeries. She takes along a written summary of what she wants to say, so that she can leave a copy with the MP. She sees the MP for ten minutes, who agrees to support the campaign to get the bypass built along Route three.

Getting it right
If there's an issue you want to raise, make sure that your MP is the right person to contact. MPs will only deal with the problems of the people they represent. MPs won't directly deal with matters dealt with by the local council or the European Union. In each case, you either need to contact your local councillor, or your local Member of the European Parliament.

Prepare exactly what you want to say. State clearly what issue you want to discuss. Make sure your statement includes:
- the key facts relating to the case
- what you want done and why
- what arguments there are to support your view.

TALK ABOUT
What have you learned from this page about how to raise an issue with your MP?

FIND OUT MORE
Research the work MPs do in Parliament and how bills become Acts of Parliament. Contact the Parliamentary Education Unit website www.explore.parliament.uk.

CHILDREN'S RIGHTS

Children and the law

In the United Kingdom there are laws to protect children's rights. There are also laws which restrict children's rights until they are considered old enough to be responsible for their own decisions.

Look at the following list and then write down what you think the legal minimum age limit is. Compare your answers with a partner's. Then check the results with your teacher.

- You can get a part-time job, provided it does not interfere with your school work.
- You can get married with your parents' consent.
- You can get a licence to drive a car.
- You can own a pet.
- You can be sent to prison.
- You can vote.
- You can be convicted of a criminal offence, if you knew you were doing something wrong.
- Your parents can get you a passport.
- You are allowed to drink alcohol in private.
- You can get a full-time job.

Time for a change in the law?

Some people think that the laws on children's rights need changing.

Parents should not be allowed to smack children. It's an excuse for violent parents to take it out on their kids.

What the law says: It is a criminal offence for anyone to physically or mentally abuse you. Your parents have the right to discipline you, but any physical punishment must not be too harsh. In Scotland, it is illegal to smack any child under three.

The law about selling tobacco to under-16s is absurd. If you want cigarettes and the shopkeeper won't sell them to you, you just get someone to buy them for you, but most of them just sell them to you anyway.

What the law says: You have to be 16 to be able to buy tobacco. Anyone who sells tobacco to someone who is underage is guilty of an offence and can be taken to court.

If your parents agree, you should be able to leave home when you are 14. Most 14-year-olds are mature enough to be able to look after themselves.

What the law says: Your parents have a duty to provide you with a home and you cannot leave home without their permission until you are 16. But if your parents cannot provide a home for you, the local authority will provide one by taking you into care.

Talk about

1. Discuss these views (right) and say whether or not you think the law needs changing. Are there any other laws about children's rights which you think need to be changed?
2. What do you think a child's responsibilities should be at the age of five? What about age ten, or age 15? Do we have different responsibilities as we grow up? What are they?

For your file »

Draw a chart showing the ages at which the law in the UK allows young people to do different things. Say whether you think any of these laws need changing and give your reasons.

Aim: To explore what your rights are and how the law protects the rights of young people in the UK.

The rights of the child

The rights of children throughout the world were set out in 1989 in the United Nations Convention on the Rights of the Child. This consists of 54 rights which every child has. These are some of the most important.

- The right to a name and to be granted a nationality.
- The right to express opinions and have these opinions considered in matters which affect their wellbeing.
- The right to freedom of thought, conscience and religion, subject to parental guidance and national law.
- Protection from all forms of physical and mental violence, neglect or maltreatment.
- Protection from employment that is likely to harm or to interfere with their development or education.
- The right to the highest standards of health and healthcare facilities.
- The right to free education at primary level.
- The right to special protection for children who are refugees, have disabilities, are orphans or from minority ethnic groups.

Check your understanding

Study the list of rights included in the UN Convention on the Rights of the Child. Do you think there are any rights that are more important than others? Why? Give reasons for your views. What other rights do you think the Convention included?

FACT FILE

Abuses of children's rights

- It is estimated that over 250 million of the world's children work. Over eight million of these children are living in slavery with no control over their lives.
- As many as ten million children around the world work in the sex industry and are regularly engaged in sex for money.
- About ten million children die each year from illnesses related to poverty and hunger. In Africa, about 10 000 children die each day from malnutrition and lack of health care.
- In many developing countries, children do not have access to education. In south-east Asia, for example, it is estimated that the number of illiterate people will double in the next 30 years.

Campaigning for children's rights

Pressure groups which exist to campaign to protect children's rights include:

- The NSPCC, or National Society for the Prevention of Cruelty to Children. The NSPCC campaigns with its Full Stop campaign, arguing that physical and mental abuse must be stamped out as soon as possible.
- Anti-Slavery International. This organization fights against children being forced to work for little or no money. They can be contacted at: Anti-Slavery International, Thomas Clarkson House, The Stableyard, Broomgrove Road, London SW9 9TL, Tel: 020 7501 8920, Fax: 020 7738 4110, website: www.antislavery.org.
- Article 12 campaigns for young people to be better represented, so that they can make decisions for themselves and help protect their own rights. Contact them at: Article 12, c/o CRAE, 94 White Lion St, London N1 9PF, Tel: 020 7278 8222, Fax: 020 7278 9552, website: www.article12.com.

For your file »

Find out about the work of the NSPCC, Anti-Slavery International or Article 12. Write a short report about their campaigns and what they are doing to try to protect children's rights.

WORLD PROBLEMS

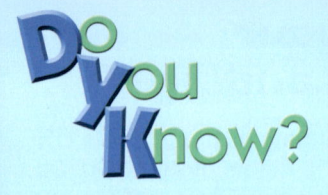

Do You Know?

What are the main problems facing the world's citizens?

Today, what goes on in one part of the world increasingly affects what goes on in another. As a result, there are a number of major problems, which are of importance to everyone on our planet, wherever they might live.

Environmental pollution

Because of human activity, we are destroying large parts of our natural environment. For example, fossil fuels like coal, oil and gas are burned for energy in developed countries. This not only causes air pollution in America, but also acid rain in Europe and global warming, which causes flooding in developing countries like Bangladesh.

Population growth

Currently, the world population stands at over six billion. However, our planet can only support so many people. As the population grows, so natural resources such as food and clean water grow scarcer. Inadequate food and water supplies lead to greater risk of famine and disease.

World health

Today, the biggest danger to world health is the spread of AIDS. Over 30 million people now have **HIV**, the virus which causes AIDS. Many of these people live in developing countries, which cannot afford the expensive drugs which may halt the spread of the disease.

In China, families are allowed only one child.

Talk About

Which of the world's problems do you think are the most serious? On your own, list the problems facing the world starting with what you think is the most serious. Then compare your lists in a group discussion.

ACTION

1. Design a survey, asking people what they think are the major issues facing the world today. Use the advice about surveys on pages 17–18 to help you. Write up the results as a report and present the report to your class.

2. Cut out articles and reports about world problems from recent newspapers and magazines. Work in a group to produce a wall display to inform people about the problems which the world faces.

> **Aim:** To understand what the main problems in the world today are and how they affect everybody.

Poverty

Many people in developing countries live in poverty – they have little or no money or possessions. Over half of the world's population live on less than $2 a day. And the gap between the world's poorest and richest people keeps on growing.

Third world debt

Many developing countries are also in debt to developed countries. Because of debt interest, the problem never goes away, despite the efforts of charities, governments and pressure groups. This means that developing countries spend money on debt repayments, rather than sorting out problems affecting their own people.

Drugs

The world drugs trade is worth over $400 billion, or around 10 per cent of total world trade. Illegal drugtaking helps fund terrorism, increases crime as people steal to fund their drug habit, and spreads AIDS through the sharing of dirty needles.

Global security

In the 21st century, two main threats exist to global security. Firstly, international terrorist groups are well-funded and well-informed – witness the terrible events on 11 September 2001 when the World Trade Center and thousands of lives were destroyed. And secondly, the spread of weapons of mass destruction (bombs, nerve agents, nuclear capabilities) means that there is an increasing chance that they will one day be used by someone somewhere.

Globalization

The world today is very different from what it was 50 years ago. A major change is occurring – countries are becoming more dependent on one another.

The earth is now a 'global village' and countries are trading much more with each other. This process, where people, businesses and countries become more reliant on each other, is called globalization. Here, what goes on at one end of the 'village' directly affects what goes on at the other.

Globalization, however, may not all be to the good. For example, if the economy in the USA – the most powerful country in the world – starts to shrink and go into recession, it would have a knock-on effect on other world economies and cause them to shrink also.

Check your understanding

1. What is meant by the terms 'globalization' and 'the global village'?
2. What developments in transport and communications have occurred in the last 50 years to make the world more of a 'global village'?

BECOMING A GLOBAL CITIZEN

Do You Know?

What does being a global citizen mean?

What does being a global citizen mean in practice? Here are some suggestions:

There's so much happening — famine in Africa, the war on terror, the growth of the internet. You need to figure out what's really important.
(Zahir, Bradford)

Our school has a link with a school in India — we video-conference with them and exchange emails and pictures. Getting to know people in other countries is the best way of understanding the issues facing everyone in the world.
(Josh, Deptford)

You need to be able to identify solutions for global problems. It's no good talking about third world debt unless you can suggest what to do about it.
(Tara, Belfast)

You should consider the consequences of your actions. For example, you respect the environment and recycle whatever you can.
(Jane, Birmingham)

You need to keep up with the news, not just in the UK, but around the world.
(Dougal, Perth)

Finding out what the United Nations and international charities like Amnesty are doing is really important.
(Sanjit, London)

Talk About

In groups, discuss these views and say what you think being a global citizen means. Then list the things you think a global citizen ought to do.

The Link Schools Programme

One way of developing your understanding of global issues is by linking your school to a school in another country. Link Community Development has a schools programme, which twins schools in the UK with schools in rural and township areas of South Africa, Ghana and Uganda.

The African schools with which Link works are very deprived and poorly resourced. The Link Schools Programme provides funding for projects to help schools in Africa meet their needs and, at the same time, helps pupils in UK schools to understand development issues.

ACTION

1. Find out more about the Link Schools Programme. Contact Link Community Development, Unit 39, Kings Exchange Business Village, Tileyard Road, London N7 9AH, website: www.lcd.org.uk.

2. Does your school have a link with any schools in the developing world? If so, find out all about the link and decide how your class can either become involved in an existing project or suggest a project that your class could develop.

3. If your school does not already have a link with a school in a developing country, prepare a proposal saying why you think it would be a good idea to develop such a link. Include in your proposal suggestions for projects that could be developed as part of the link programme and list the benefits there would be both for your school and your partner school.

AIM — To explore what it means to be a global citizen and how to research a global issue.

HOW TO... research a global issue

Becoming a global citizen involves developing your understanding of global problems and what can be done about them. You and your classmates can do this by researching global issues and then discussing them. You can find out information on a global issue in a number of ways.

- You can use the internet (see below).
- You can obtain information from books, newspapers, magazines and CDs from the school's resources centre and the local library.
- You can also get information by contacting pressure groups and charities. For example, if you are researching environmental issues, you can contact Friends of the Earth and Greenpeace. If you are researching population issues, you can contact Population Concern. If you are researching poverty, you can contact Oxfam and War on Want.

First, choose the issue you wish to research. Then make a list of the information you wish to find out and the questions you need to answer. Your list should include:

- what the problem is and how widespread is it
- where the problem occurs and who is affected by it
- what the main causes of the problem are
- why it is necessary to do something about it
- who is trying to solve the problem and what they are doing
- what else needs to be done to solve the problem.

Getting information from the internet

1. Make a list of any internet sites you already know that contain good information.
2. Choose a good search engine. Use it to search for sites which can give you the information you require. Popular search engines include www.yahoo.co.uk and www.google.co.uk.
3. Look at your search results. If your search produces too much information, you may need to narrow your search. You can do this by being more specific about the information you require.
4. Make a list of the sites that appear the most useful. Check how old the information is, and how much use each site will be to you.
5. Pick the top three, four or five internet sites, and research them in detail. When finding out information, make a note of:
   - the source of your information
   - the date the information was published
   - what is being said
   - how relevant it is to your research
   - any new information you now feel you need to research
   - any other internet sites you can visit, or contacts you can email for further information.
6. Cross-reference your information. This includes checking that the information from one site agrees with the information from another.
7. Review all of your information. If you still have any gaps, go back to stages 1 and 2 and repeat them.

FIND OUT MORE

In order to deal with global issues and manage the world community, an increasing number of international organizations have been created over the last 50 years. These include the United Nations, the European Union and the North Atlantic Treaty Organization (NATO). Find out about one of these organizations and write a paragraph about it for your file.

ACTION — Choose a global issue and research it. Write up the information you find out in a short report and present this to the rest of the class.

DEBATING GLOBAL ISSUES

Putting your point of view

Peter is going to take part in a debate on world poverty. He decides he wants to argue that more needs to be done to help poorer developing countries. Here is a draft of a speech he has prepared.

> Do you know that every four seconds a child dies in one of the world's developing countries? That's over seven and a half million children a year.
>
> The main reason why these children die is poverty. They are dying from hunger because they can't get enough to eat. They are dying from diseases spread in dirty water, because they haven't a clean water supply. They are dying from illnesses, such as measles, because they don't have access to the healthcare that could prevent such diseases.
>
> The situation is worst in Africa. In Malawi, many children cannot get the education that would help to lift them out of poverty because they don't go to school. They are too busy looking for clean water or begging for food. In Botswana, AIDS is so widespread that huge numbers of the population will die in the next 20 years.
>
> In many African countries there are armed conflicts. Children as young as six are involved in the fighting and huge sums of money are spent on arms rather than on tackling poverty.
>
> People in developed countries should do more to help prevent world poverty. We should stop manufacturing and exporting arms to the developing world. The Government should increase the amount of money it sends in aid. If you were living in poverty, you'd want rich countries to help you!
>
> Some people argue that African governments only waste the money that is given to them. But we could channel the aid through charities to make sure it reaches the people who really need it.
>
> To sum up, the world faces a humanitarian crisis that we must do something about. Too many children are dying. People say we live in a global village. As global citizens, it's our responsibility to help those in the world who are to poor to be able to help themselves.

HOW TO... argue a viewpoint

1. Grab the audience's attention. Start with a dramatic statement or question that gets the audience's attention.
2. Develop your arguments logically. Once you have introduced your argument, develop it. Go into more detail. Bring in other issues that support your argument. Give a clear list of reasons why people should agree with you.
3. Support your arguments with facts and statistics. Make sure you have researched your arguments beforehand. This is so you have facts and statistics to support your arguments.
4. Include lists of three. This is a trick of public speaking. The idea is to put points in groups of three to make them easier to remember.
5. Undermine the opposition's case. Explain why the arguments against your point of view are flawed.
6. Involve the audience. Addressing the audience directly can help to win their support for your viewpoint. For example, ask them: 'How would you feel if it were you?' or involve them in what needs to be done: 'What we need to do is...'
7. At the end summarize your main argument, and the reasons that support it. End with a flourish about what needs to be done and who needs to do it.

AIM Consider how to argue a viewpoint and take part in a debate on a global issue.

A class debate

As a class, organize a debate on your own motion, or one of the following motions:

> This house believes that nuclear energy is the best way to stop us polluting the planet with fossil fuels.

> This house believes that everyone in the UK should give a penny in each pound they earn towards reducing poverty in the developing world.

> This house believes that war can never be justified.

HOW TO... deliver a speech

There are a number of things you can do when making a speech in a debate which will help you to get your points across.

- Make eye contact. Keeping in touch with your audience by maintaining eye contact is a good way of ensuring that they pay attention to what you are saying.
- Vary your tone of voice. If you speak in the same tone of voice it can become monotonous and boring for your listeners.
- Speak up and don't mumble. Make sure you speak loudly enough to be heard at the back of the room and don't drop your voice at the end of a sentence or the end of your speech.
- Maintain an even pace. If you speak either too slowly or too quickly the audience will eventually 'switch off'.
- Stand up and don't slouch. Body language is important. No matter how nervous you are feeling, try to look confident.
- Use dramatic pauses. Skilled speakers use pauses as a way of stressing key points and making their speeches more dramatic.

TALK ABOUT

After the debate, discuss who gave the best speech and why. Talk about how well the argument was developed and how well the speech was delivered. Use the checklists of how to argue a viewpoint and how to deliver a speech to help you to decide whose speech was the most effective.

Check your understanding

Study Peter's draft on page 40 and the advice on how to argue a viewpoint above. Discuss how successfully Peter presents his argument. Does he make a good start? How well does he develop and support his argument? Does he succeed in undermining the opposition's case and involving the audience? Does he give a good summary of his arguments and have an emphatic ending? Suggest how he might improve his argument.

THE MEDIA – NEWS STORIES

Reading between the lines

We rely on the media for information about what is going on in the world. We watch television news bulletins to keep up-to-date with the latest news. We read about events and the background to them in national and local newspapers. Instant news updates are available on the internet.

However, a news story can be presented in many different ways. When a news story only presents one point of view, it is said to have **bias**. This can sometimes be easy or difficult to detect. So when you read a news story you need to be able to 'read between the lines'.

Business hails 2002 environment summit a 'huge success'

From TV News

Big business has declared the Environment Summit held in Johannesburg, South Africa, an 'outstanding success'.

A spokesman for UK Oil Corp said: "The summit has taken an excellent view towards improving the global environment. By working together, big business and governments around the world will be able to obtain economic growth. This will give us the funds to help clean up the environment."

The summit agreed a range of voluntary measures to help the environment. A leading New Zealand politician said: "It is good that some measures were agreed."

Pressure groups such as Greenpeace and Friends of the Earth also attended the summit.

The summit was clearly a success, and we should congratulate our world leaders for taking the right action.

HOW TO... detect bias

There are several different ways that bias can be added to a story. These include:
- leaving out key facts
- misquoting people by leaving out part of what they have said
- not quoting those people who disagree with you
- making supportive statements without backing them up with evidence
- using photos to support a particular point of view.

One way of detecting bias is to look for a pattern, which gives a story a particular point of view. This is known as giving a story 'spin'. Another way is to compare how several newspapers, news channels, or internet sites report the same story.

Giving it a spin

Notice how the report is written so that there is a bias towards businesses and their point of view of the summit.

1 Strong emotion language is used, to support the author's point of view.

2 The report makes no mention of the fact that it is big business which caused much of the environmental pollution in the first place.

3 None of the environmental groups who attended are quoted in this report.

4 The New Zealand politician could have easily added: "However, what is needed is not voluntary measures, but a clear plan of action that will force the developed countries of the world to act." This gives his quote a very different meaning.

5 A broad statement with no facts to back it up.

6 This picture could easily have been of the African protesters who were at the summit, who disagreed with what happened.

AIM To understand how news stories are presented, what bias is and how to detect it.

Here are two other news stories. They show how the Environment Summit could have been reported very differently.

Opportunity wasted

From the Environment News internet site, sponsored by the Southern Earth Alliance.

Opportunity wasted. That's what happened in Johannesburg last weekend.

Another day, another summit. Another excuse for delegates to travel to a foreign country. Another reason for the press to follow them.

And did anything actually get achieved? How much did the government spend on this summit? And how much pollution did it cause?

One thing is clear – something has to be done about the environment.

Global warming, massive flooding, widescale droughts. Too much water in some parts of the globe. Not enough in others. It's time for action.

A start would be enough of these summits.

Southern Earth Alliance has always stood up for the environment.

Now we ask that our Government does the same. By scrapping these useless summits. By listening to ordinary people.

And, above all, by taking some real action.

Mixed views from environment summit

From the *Daily Globe* newspaper

A mixed view – that was the verdict of last weekend's Environment Summit.

The summit, held in Johannesburg, contained a mixture of governments, interested businesses and pressure groups. There were some hopes that the governments would adopt new pollution targets.

True, big business managed to ensure that most of these targets were voluntary. UK Oil Corp called this 'a sensible view'. We note, however, that UK Oil Corp will be free to ignore these targets if they wish.

But for the first time, the mood appears to be changing. An opinion poll released at the weekend showed a rise for an environment tax in developed countries. And pressure groups like Friends of the Earth and Greenpeace are gaining more and more support.

TALK ABOUT

1. Study the news story on page 42. It illustrates one way that the 2002 Environment Summit could have been reported. Discuss what bias is. What are the different ways a person can give bias to a story? What is the best way to detect bias?

2. Compare the three news reports. What impressions of the Environment Summit does each one give? Whose point of view is the story told from? List the major differences between the three reports.

3. Discuss your findings. Are you surprised by them? If so, why? How has this exercise affected your understanding of the way news is reported by the media?

FIND OUT MORE

1. Look at the way several newspapers, internet sites, or different television channels report the same story. Can you find any bias?

2. Compare a newspaper, a television channel's news bulletin and an internet news site. What are the differences in the way the news is reported?

UNDERSTANDING THE MEDIA - PICTURES

The power of pictures

Today, pictures are more powerful than ever before. In the last few years, technology has increased to bring us more and more images in different ways. We can now watch videos on the internet, and even send and receive images on our mobile phones.

The media frequently use still images to show what is occurring in a news story. Usually, these images illustrate a particular side to a news story. Because of this, an image can be used to give a story bias.

TALK ABOUT

Look at photographs 1 to 3, which show the Earth Summit in Johannesburg.

Pick one of the photographs, and answer the following questions.

1. What do you first think when you look at the photograph?
2. What do you think the most important thing in the photograph is?
3. Do you think the photograph is positive, negative or neutral?
4. Do you think any of the photos are biased? If so, in what way?

Captions

A **caption** is the sentence under a photograph, which explains what it is. A good caption is short, clear and helps to tell the story. Because they help you interpret the photo, captions can be used to create and reinforce bias.

Here are three possible captions for photograph 1:

a) *British Prime Minister Tony Blair with President Chirac of France during the Earth Summit in Johannesburg.*

b) *Representatives of the environmentalist organizations staged a walk out from the Earth Summit in Johannesburg.*

c) *South African President Thabo Mbeki, addresses the Earth Summit in Johannesburg.*

TALK ABOUT

1. Study the three captions. What do you think of each caption? Do any of the captions change what you think of the photograph? Which caption do you think best fits the photo? Why?
2. Look at photographs 2 and 3. Imagine you had to write your own caption for an adult newspaper. What would you say?
3. Now imagine you had to write a caption for the same photos, but for a children's news magazine. Would your captions change? Why? Give reasons for your views.

AIM — To understand how pictures are used in the media and how they can create bias.

The full picture

Pictures can also be manipulated, to change to their size and colour. For example, look at photos 4 and 5. Photo 4 shows the complete picture. But photo 5 only shows part of the picture. This is known as cropping the picture.

4

5

Members of Friends of the Earth stage a 'small' demonstration at the Earth Summit.

ACTION

1. Choose a current news story. Look at the pictures that are used to illustrate it in newspapers, magazines and on the internet. Cut out three or four examples of different pictures and captions connected to the same news stories. In small groups in class, discuss what you think of each picture. Is there any bias?

   Alternatively, find three or four different pictures and captions of the same news story. Cut off the captions and copy them out so that you can't tell which caption goes with which picture. Show them to a partner. Can they match the captions to the pictures?

2. Cut out three or four powerful pictures you find in newspapers, magazines or on the internet. Write about why they are powerful. Comment on the captions used and suggest alternative captions for them.

TALK ABOUT

1. What effect does changing a photo from colour to black and white have? What effect does cropping photo 5 have? Which do you prefer? Why?

2. Look back at photos 1, 2 and 3. What do you think is going on outside of each of the photographs? Do you think a photograph can ever tell a complete story or not? Why?

FIND OUT MORE

Contact a photographer at a local newspaper. Arrange for them to visit your class to show you some of their pictures. Interview them to find out more about what they are looking for when they take a picture, and how they select their best photos from those they have taken.

45

BEING A VOLUNTEER

Getting involved supporting others

Being an active citizen means getting involved in helping other people in the community. You may already be doing what is called **volunteering** – giving up some of your time for free to support others. For example, you may be caring for a member of your family at home. Or you may be translating for a member of the community who doesn't speak English.

Alternatively, you may want to volunteer to do some work for an organization which offers support. Many people choose to work as volunteers at some point in their lives. There are several different advantages to volunteering. In particular, you can gain real experience working with people, and increase your skills.

Volunteers can be permanent or temporary – it's up to you. There are a vast range of organizations that people choose to volunteer for, including charities, societies, clubs and pressure groups.

What makes a good voluntary experience?

In order for a voluntary placement to work, both the organization and the individual should gain from it. When searching for volunteers, organizations look for the following characteristics:
- some free time
- an ability to get on with people
- an interest in what the organization does
- enthusiasm and energy
- the ability to learn new skills.

In return, the organization should provide the volunteer with the opportunity to grow, learn new skills and have fun. Following a survey of young people, the Institute of Voluntary Research published a list of what makes a good voluntary placement.

A good voluntary placement should be:
- flexible
- easy to access – it should be nearby
- provide good incentives – this could include public recognition, some sort of reward, or maybe some training that will help you later in life
- varied
- well organized
- fun
- legitimate.

The last point is particularly important. As citizens, we should all become involved in campaigning for the things that we want. However, some pressure groups encourage their volunteers to become involved in civil disobedience. This is when members of a pressure group break the law in order to help further their aims. For example, some groups, which are campaigning against the development of genetically-modified crops, encourage their members to take part in activities in which the crops are damaged and destroyed. This action is against the law. It goes against the idea of responsible action, in which you make a protest but the protest is within the law.

TALK ABOUT

Do you know anyone who is a volunteer? Do you do any voluntary work yourself? If so, why do you do it, and what do you get out of it?

Check your understanding

What are the features of a good voluntary placement? Talk about what a volunteer should hope to get out of a placement and what the organization should hope to get out of a volunteer.

AIM To explore what it means to be a volunteer, and what makes a good voluntary position.

HOW TO... volunteer

1. Choose the organization that you want to work for.
2. Find out if the organization has any vacancies. If they do, research whether they would be suitable for you.
3. Make a clear list of what you would be willing to do. This should include what tasks you feel you would be capable of, and how much time you would be able to give.
4. Decide what you want to get out of the experience. This could include:
   - a sense of reward from helping others
   - an opportunity to meet new people
   - training and the opportunity to develop new skills
   - experience in doing a particular job, which will help you later in life.
5. Find out as much about the organization as you can, including whom you should contact if you want to become a volunteer.
6. Contact the organization you want to volunteer for, either by phone, email or letter. Explain who you are, why you want to help and what sort of help you would be able to offer.

Becoming a volunteer

Gemma decided she wanted to become a volunteer for her local Oxfam group. She particularly liked the idea of working to help people in the developing world.

She contacted the organization. They said that there was an Oxfam shop in her area which needed volunteers.

Gemma made a list of what she would be willing to do. This included talking to people, working on a computer and getting experience of working in a shop. She'd also be willing to do some fundraising, with some training.

Gemma contacted the local Oxfam shop. Speaking to the manager of the shop on the phone, she agreed to help out sorting items that people donate to the shop for a couple of hours after school each week. Although this is not exactly what she hoped to do, Gemma agreed, as she felt it would be a good way to start and might lead to further opportunities.

TALK ABOUT

Talk about different voluntary work that you could do for the local community. What sort of voluntary work do you think you would be most suitable for? Say why you would or would not be willing to do some voluntary work during the next summer holidays.

ACTION

1. Talk to your school, and any clubs, societies or pressure groups that you belong to or are interested in. Have a look in your local newspaper and on the internet. Find a voluntary position that interests you, and get involved.
2. Contact Millennium Volunteers at www.millenniumvolunteers.gov.uk. Look at the different voluntary posts available. Are there any posts that interest you? Why?
3. Keep a diary of any voluntary work that you do. Record what was particularly rewarding, and why you enjoyed it. Also record what you would do to make the experience better, and what you have learned from the experience.

GLOSSARY

Antisocial behaviour
Actions which damage the community (page 14).

Bias
When a story only presents a certain point of view (page 42).

Canvassing
Interviewing people to find out how they will vote and to persuade them to vote for a certain party. (page 30).

Caption
The sentence under a photograph, which explains what the photo is about (page 44).

Charity
An organization that exists to help people, which raises voluntary funds (page 12).

Constituency
The area that an MP represents. The people who vote for the MP in this area are called constituents (page 30).

Electoral register
The list of people in an area who can vote (page 26).

HIV
The virus that causes AIDS, which leads to a person's immune system breaking down (page 36).

Hustings
A meeting so people can ask candidates in an election what they would do if they were elected (page 30).

Manifesto
The things that a political party would do if it was the Government (page 28).

Political party
A group of people who share similar ideas about how the country should be governed (page 28).

Racism
Unfairly discriminating against a person or group of people, just because of their race (page 24).

Responsibility
Something that you should do, for example we all have the responsibility to report crime when we see it (page 7).

Returning officer
The official responsible for organizing an election (page 30).

Right
Something that you are entitled to, for example the right to work (page 6).

School council
A committee of representatives which meets to discuss school issues (page 8).

Stereotyping
Unfairly creating an image of a group of people behaving in the same way (page 23).

Volunteering
Giving up some of your time for free (page 46).

YMP (Youth Member of Parliament)
A member of the Parliament that represents young people aged 17 and below (page 26).